WHY SHOULD I TITHE?

NCOVERING THE TRUTH ABOUT
THING

HENRY D. DANIELS

ANGE PUBLISHING, LLC
BROKE PINES, FLORIDA

Orange Publishing, LLC
15757 Pines Blvd. Suite 245
Pembroke Pines, Florida 33027

Unless otherwise indicated, Bible quotations are taken frc
King James Version of the Bible.

Book Layout ©2013 BookDesignTemplates.com

Cover Design: Bryan Edwards

Edited By: Sharyn Kopf

Why Should I Tithe?/ Henry D. Daniels. —1st ed.
ISBN 978-0-9975394-0-0

CONTENTS

i

Dedication & Appreciation

I would like to dedicate this book to my wife Teresa. You are my beautiful, wonderful, awesome, fantastic partner in marriage and ministry and more importantly the love of my life. Without your understanding of me and my call your love, support, and motivation, this book would have never become a reality. Thank you for truly being my good thing! In addition, I dedicate this book to our son Christopher, who currently serves in the United States Coast Guard. You are a wonderful son of whom I am proud. Thank you for supporting me in my ministry endeavors.

I would like to also thank Cornerstone Christian Center Church. I have been blessed by God with you. I truly pastor with joy.

No one person achieves anything without the impact and influences of others. Since committing my life to the Lord, every Pastor that I have served, has made an indelible impact on my life. Thank you for giving yourselves to the Lord. I am the beneficiary of you answering the call to ministry. Thank you for teaching, training and praying.

*And ye shall know the truth, and the truth
shall make you free.*

—John 8:32

Introduction

Most of us have tried on clothes at a retail apparel store. You take a look in the mirror then, wanting more feedback, ask the sales associate, "How do I look?"

The typical response is usually in the affirmative. "Oh, that fits you so well" or "It really brings out your eyes" or "That looks great on you." It might be nice to hear such words, but you know deep down something doesn't seem right. Sure, the sales associate said it looks fine, but the mirror says you're a hot mess. Yet the employee is the professional; she should know. So you go on her word and make the purchase.

Then you get home and try it on again, only to discover it looks horrible. At that moment you wish the sales associate would have had the guts to tell you the truth before you spent the money. That truth would have freed you to find the right garment. The employee told you what she thought you wanted to hear to make the sale. That associate's motive was fueled by the sales commission she would earn.

Most people in most situations want the truth. We want the truth because that is how we measure trustworthiness. If you don't tell me the truth you can't be trusted. If I don't tell you the truth you won't trust me.

We want the truth because lies are so prevalent today. Many people don't mind telling white lies and falsehoods.

We want the truth because with truth comes clarity. I can make better decisions when I am armed with the truth.

I approach this topic and every topic I write or speak about on the platform of telling the truth. In this book, I am simply sharing what I have discovered concerning tithing. I don't have any other motive but to explore this truth so the reader can be free to please God with his life.

Still, I am concerned about what I share because one day I will have to answer for all I write and speak. With the gravity of being responsible for my words, on my mind I wrote Why Should I Tithe?

Join me as we uncover the truth about tithing. May it lead you to a new perspective on this important subject.

[1]

Why I Wrote This Book

After my salvation experience in 1981, I had so many questions about the Bible. You see, for the first eighteen years of my life—from the early sixties to 1980—my parents made sure my brother, two sisters and I were in church every Sunday morning. Week after week, we awoke early enough to attend Sunday school, followed by about fifteen minutes to get a quick bite to eat in the fellowship hall. Then we headed to the sanctuary for the morning worship service.

During those formative years of my life, through all the Sunday school lessons and church sermons, I cannot recall anyone mentioning the word "tithe." Can you believe that? Not one statement about tithing in any service or Sunday school class! Yes, they talked about membership dues, general offerings and auxiliary fund-raising efforts. But tithing was not mentioned at all.

Then, after eighteen years of going to this church, I made Jesus my Lord and Savior at another church. That's right, almost two decades of going to my parent's church and I was not born again. Since I accepted Jesus as Lord at this new church, I decided to make it my spiritual home. That's where I first heard the term "tithe." I not only heard the term there, but the pastor referred to Scriptures that actually mention tithing.

At this point, I was faced with a question: Does this tithe thing apply to believers today? During my research, I discovered many Christians want to know the answer as well.

To find it, I needed to do an intense study on the subject of tithing. My heart's cry as a brand-new believer was to only engage in activities that please God. I researched and studied and researched and studied some more to be 100 percent certain I got this right. If I am going to give money to my church, I want to make sure God is pleased with what I give and how I give it.

I WANT MY GIVING TO PLEASE GOD.

Tithing is often misunderstood among Christians and non- Christians alike because many believers do not know how to "rightly divide" the Word of God.

Study to shew thyself approved unto God, a workman that needeth not to be ashamed, rightly dividing the word of truth
—2 Timothy 2:15

"Rightly divide" simply means the ability to properly interpret Scripture. The incorrect interpretation of the Word of God will produce an incorrect application. In other words, if we don't interpret the Bible correctly we won't apply it correctly. And by not applying the Word of God correctly, it is very likely there will be areas in our lives where we will fail to please Him. We may be sincere in our efforts, but we will be sincerely wrong.

Tithing is also misunderstood because there are some pastors and so-called Bible teachers who teach from a non-biblical perspective on the subject. Some pastors have adopted a secular worldview that causes a misinterpretation of Scripture.

Instead of approaching it from a neutral perspective to extract the truths from the Word, some approach the Bible by reading and interpreting it through their preconceived philosophical lens. It is a shame that some pastors and teachers feel the need to adopt unbiblical, philosophical views in an attempt to reach their un-churched communities. We can effectively reach our communities with the gospel without compromising biblical truths.

Of course, many biblical truths and concepts will not be understood when we approach them without setting our minds to be in agreement with the Word of God. Consider the following verse:

And be not conformed to this world: but be ye transformed by the renewing of your mind, that ye may prove what is that good, and acceptable, and perfect, will of God

—Romans 12:2

To grasp this verse, I like to analyze it in reverse. The objective here is to prove, determine or verify what God's will is for our lives. Many people are searching for His will in their families, in their careers and even in their relationships with others.

However, the process of determining God's will requires one to be transformed by renewing the mind. This transformation is simply changing the way we think about things—literally, an adjustment in how we view life. This change cannot be "conformed to this world." Conforming means being squeezed into a philosophical lens of society that contradicts the Bible. Whew!

Now that we have analyzed that verse let's put it all together in one simple statement:

When my philosophical view of the situations I face in life contradict Scripture, I will choose to permit the Bible to override my philosophy. By doing this I am renewing my mind. Only then can I determine what God really wants me to do in different situations.

Let me say it another way—the Word of God will become my final authority in life!

Please understand this. As long as we attempt to comprehend spiritual things with the philosophy, ideas and concepts commonly accepted in our society, we will not grasp the realm of the spirit.

But the natural, non-spiritual man does not accept or welcome or admit into his heart the gifts and teachings and revelations of the Spirit of God, for they are folly (meaningless nonsense) to him; and he is incapable of knowing them [of progressively recognizing, understanding, and becoming better acquainted with them] because they are spiritually discerned and estimated and appreciated.

—1 Corinthians 2:14 (AMP)

From this verse it becomes even clearer that a person who is not spiritual will not accept the teachings of God because those spiritual concepts and philosophies can only be spiritually appreciated. I see this so frequently in the media.

For instance, a reporter will ask a question concerning Scripture and when a pastor or sound Bible teacher answers, the reporter will have a puzzled look on his face. The reporter's body language and facial expression communicates disbelief to the viewer. Many times the disbelief is really unbelief because the answer given requires spiritual discernment. If one wants to understand biblical concepts then receiving salvation and becoming born of the Spirit is needed.

Many people reject any teaching that supports tithing because they suspect the teacher has an ulterior motive. Some believe the teaching is only presented to raise funds for the church.

I wrote this book to share the results of my personal research and study on tithing, which I completed prior to accepting a position in full-time ministry. I do not view myself as a theologian or Bible scholar but as a normal, everyday Christian who desires to please God with his life. It's not for my benefit. I only hope you, the reader, will discover how to please God with scriptural giving.

Wisdom is the principal thing; therefore get wisdom: and with all thy getting get understanding.
—Proverbs 4:7

Everyone will agree that knowledge is extremely important in life. Yet wisdom is more important. Wisdom can be defined as "the ability to apply knowledge." What good would it be to have all the knowledge in the world and not know how to apply it for your benefit?

Wisdom, then, must be of the highest rank because with wisdom we gain understanding. I hope you will not only gain that understanding but be able to properly interpret the often-difficult scriptural principles contained in the Old Testament.

With that in mind, I will quote multiple passages in the hope of making those principles easier to grasp.

APPROACHING HIM WITH CONFIDENCE.

Let us therefore come boldly unto the throne of grace, that we may obtain mercy, and find grace to help in time of need
—Hebrews 4:16

This passage encourages us to "come boldly unto the throne of grace." Such a bold approach to God's throne can be referred to as confidence, a primary element in faith. Also, when we approach God with this confidence, we gain mercy and grace. We absolutely need to come to God with confidence in prayer.

When we give to the Lord, we are coming before His throne. Giving to God's work requires scriptural confidence. Your confidence in your giving will rise to new heights as you walk in this practical principle of tithing.

[2]

Should I obey the Old Testament?

Wow, what a topic to address! Many believers struggle with this intricate, theological question because there are so many different perspectives and opinions concerning the Old Testament.

After my salvation experience, I never gave much thought as to which Testament to obey. I simply read the Bible, Old and New Testaments, and if it stated to do something or not do something I tried to obey.

Then I ran into Scriptures in the Old Testament that gave me chills. Passages about things like bringing animals into the worship facility to offer as a bloody sacrifice. Can you imagine a church today where live animals would be killed as a sacrifice?

I began to understand not every Scripture in the Old Testament pertains to believers today, which is one reason some Christians believe they only need to obey and adhere to the tenets and principles of the New Testament. It certainly seems easier.

Of course, the New Testament says we should love our enemies and that's definitely not easy!

OLD OR NEW TESTAMENT BELIEVER?

I've heard Christians say, "I'm a New Testament believer; the Old Testament doesn't apply to me." Yet those same Christians would quote Scriptures contained in the Old Testament.

Several years ago, a book popularized the prayer of Jabez, and it was widely quoted among many Christians.

And Jabez called on the God of Israel, saying, "Oh that thou wouldest bless me indeed, and enlarge my coast, and that thine hand might be with me, and that thou wouldest keep me from evil, that it may not grieve me!" And God granted him that which he requested.

—1 Chronicles 4:10

This prayer was popular in every denomination and even among non-denominationalists. But if we say the Old Testament doesn't apply to our lives, then we should not believe in or even quote this passage, especially in a prayer.

Years ago, a gospel music group recorded a song with the lyrics, "I'm blessed in the city, I'm blessed in the field, I'm blessed when I come and when I go ..." These lyrics were extracted from Deuteronomy 28 ... in the Old Testament. Yet those New Testament Christians were singing it fervently! I can cite many more examples, but I think you get the picture. Passages in the Old Testament still apply to us today!

Yet even with that admission, some believers have adopted the method of excluding anything in the Old Testament "law." Those believers stand on Galatians 3:13.

Christ hath redeemed us from the curse of the law, being made a curse for us: for it is written, Cursed is every one that hangeth on a tree.

—Galatians 3:13

Yes, we need to remember that some statements in the law absolutely do not apply to Christians today. But some that do apply are contained in the law but are not exclusive to the law.

When a young man asked Jesus what he needed to do to inherit eternal life, Jesus quoted some of the commandments in Mark 10:17-19. According to Jesus, portions of the Old Testament, especially in the law, should be adhered to by Christians today.

As a matter of fact, I strongly urge children to honor their mother and father so "their days may be long on the earth" (Exod. 20:12). I agree with the law that we should not kill another human being or steal from someone. Also, know that you have angels to protect and deliver you because you reverence the Lord (Ps. 34:7). The Old Testament and even portions of the law are beneficial today!

> *All Scripture is given by inspiration of God, and is profitable for doctrine, for reproof, for correction, for instruction in righteousness.*
>
> —2 Timothy 3:16

The passage above says "all Scripture is given by inspiration of God..." This portion of the verse makes several points.

First, all Scripture is "God-inspired." Which means every portion of the Bible—the words, the narratives, the prophecies—are all as God saw fit for them to be.

Second, because "all Scripture" is as God wants it to be, then we must respect each and every passage as divine.

Third, all portions of Scripture are profitable and useful in any period of time.

So, here it is in the New Testament that all of God's Word is profitable for the believer today. While we may not adhere to it by the letter of the law, there are principles in the Old and New Testaments that are beneficial for us today.

TITHING DID NOT BEGIN WITH THE LAW.

Yes, tithing is mentioned in the law. But it didn't begin there. Genesis 14:17-20 records how Abram gave tithes of all he received to Melchizedek, the king and priest. At that time, there was no scriptural law to tithe, no scriptural commandment to tithe, no scriptural compulsion to tithe. Yet, Abram thought it necessary. It's possible the principle of tithing was customary at this time, yet this was before the law was established. In other words, the principle of tithing was established long before the law.

Woe unto you, scribes and Pharisees, hypocrites! for ye pay tithe of mint and anise and cumin, and have omitted the weightier matters of the law, judgment, mercy, and faith: these ought ye to have done, and not to leave the other undone.

—Matthew 23:23

Here Jesus speaks out against the scribes and Pharisees who tithe but have no judgment, mercy or faith. However, Jesus did not stop there. He went on to say they should have these qualities but, at the end of the verse, He added they were "not to leave the other undone."

Jesus is saying to add judgment, mercy and faith to your principle of tithing, not to stop tithing. With this statement in Matthew 23:23, we learn it is God's will that the principle of tithing should not be limited to the law or the Old Testament. New Testament believers should tithe also.

For this reason, individuals who tithe today do so not by law or by commandment but by principle.

[3]

The Intervention Principle

Did you know that in order for God to intervene in your life, you must invite Him in? Yes, it's true—God will not intervene in anyone's life without their permission. You see, my friend, God does not invade or intrude in a person's life. As a matter of fact, God will not get involved in earth's affairs without man giving Him permission.

I know what you're thinking—but He's God. God is omnipotent—all-powerful. God is omnipresent—everywhere at the same time. God is omniscient—all-knowing. He can do whatever He wants to do. But once the omnipotent, omnipresent, omniscient God places something in a man's hand, He will not intervene without permission. Let's look at Scripture:

And God said, "Let us make man in our image, after our like-
ness: and let them have dominion over the fish of the sea, and
over the fowl of the air, and over the cattle, and over all the
earth, and over every creeping thing that creepeth upon the
earth."
So God created man in His own image, in the image of God
created He him; male and female created He them. And God
blessed them, and God said unto them, "Be fruitful, and mul-
tiply, and replenish the earth, and subdue it: and have do-
minion over the fish of the sea, and over the fowl of the air,
and over every living thing that moveth upon the earth."

—Genesis 1:26-28

In this passage, God created mankind, then trans-
ferred authority over earth's affairs into man's hands.
He gave man dominion over the fish, the animals, the
birds, virtually over all the earth. That word "dominion" is key. God literally gave mankind authority over
the earth. So, if anything was to occur in the earth,
man was now responsible for managing and govern-
ing it.

WHEN GOD WANTS TO INTERVENE, HE NEEDS PER-
MISSION.

Anytime God wants to intervene in the earth, He
needs a man or a woman to give Him permission or
access. Perhaps you're thinking—but what about the
flood?

According to Genesis 6:5, the flood came as a result of man's "wickedness" and "evil." The depravity of man's sin resulted in a negative reaction called judgment, which came in the form of the flood. Mankind actually invited God to judge their unbridled wickedness and evil.

"The people of the land have used oppression, and exercised robbery, and have vexed the poor and needy: yea, they have oppressed the stranger wrongfully.
"And I sought for a man among them, that should make up the hedge, and stand in the gap before me for the land, that I should not destroy it: but I found none. Therefore have I poured out mine indignation upon them; I have consumed them with the fire of my wrath: their own way have I recompensed upon their heads," saith the Lord God. ...
—Ezekiel 22:29-31

In these verses, the people's actions led to judgment. Yet God did not want to pour out judgment. So, He looked for someone who would "make up the hedge and stand in the gap" for the land.

"Stand in the gap" is used to illustrate someone interceding in prayer for another. God was looking for someone to pray to Him and ask Him not to judge the land. That act of prayer would give Him the permission He needed to intervene. But He found none, therefore judgment was poured out. How often in life—my life and your life—does God want to intervene and help, but we refused to give Him access by asking Him to do so in prayer?

ACTIONS CAUSE CONSEQUENCES.

Newton's third law of motion states: "For every action there is an equal and opposite re-action." While this is a widely accepted law of physics, I've come to realize that actions in general causes re-actions or consequences. In other words, there are consequences for my actions.

My actions in the natural realm can cause consequences in the natural realm. If I consistently choose to eat foods that are high in triglycerides and cholesterol and refuse to exercise, it is very likely I will end up with clogged arteries. My actions and choices will cause the consequences.

In the same vein, my actions in the realm of the spirit can cause consequences in both the natural and in the spirit. If I want God to give me a favorable consequence, then I must act by inviting Him into my affairs.

Job 36:11-12 states that if we obey the Lord, there will be positive consequences: "days in prosperity and years in pleasure."

If we choose to not obey the Lord, though, there will be negative consequences: "perishing by the sword."

Our actions can get God involved in our lives either positively or negatively. We have seen over and over again in the Scriptures that if we want God to intervene in our affairs we must invite Him, or give Him permission. **Remember this powerful principle!** With this one intervention principle, your life can radically change. You can begin to intentionally invite God to intervene in your life!

Yea, they turned back and tempted God, and limited the Holy One of Israel.

—Psalm 78:41

Think about that verse for a moment. The children of Israel, while they were in the wilderness, "limited the Holy One of Israel." The first time I read this verse I almost could not believe it. How can mortal man "limit" the immortal God? Yet that is exactly what the Scripture says. God may desire to operate in our lives, and we can prevent Him from doing so.

A limit is a boundary or a border. It is a fenced-in or walled-off area that we will not permit someone or something to cross. When God is limited in a person's life, He cannot fulfill His purpose in and through their life.

Please understand this about God: He is a gentleman. He never forces anyone to do anything for Him. Still, life goes better when we obey God. Jonah found that out while he was inside the belly of the whale. Once Jonah made a decision to obey God, his life started improving.

Begin to obey God and invite Him to intervene in your life and watch miracles begin to happen!

[4]

Are Christians Obligated To Tithe?

Before we seek to answer this question, we need to examine the scriptural principles concerning giving to God in general. Remember, when I give money to my church, charitable organization or to someone personally, I want to make sure, as much as possible, that God is pleased with my giving.

Let's take a look at the very first offering recorded in Scripture:

In the course of time Cain brought some of the fruits of the soil as an offering to the Lord. And Abel also brought an offering—fat portions from some of the firstborn of his flock.

The Lord looked with favor on Abel and his offering, but on Cain and his offering He did not look with favor. So Cain was very angry, and his face was downcast.

Then the Lord said to Cain, "Why are you angry? Why is your face downcast? If you do what is right, will you not be accepted? But if you do not do what is right, sin is crouching at your door; it desires to have you, but you must rule over it."
—Genesis 4:3-7 (NIV)

Both Cain and Abel brought offerings to the Lord. Both gave what they had. And, on the surface, both appear to be perfectly acceptable sacrifices.

Cain was a grain farmer, so he brought some of what the ground produced. Abel was an animal herder, so he brought what the animals produced. Again, everything appears to be fine until we see how the Lord accepted one offering and did not accept the other.

The reason God did not favor one offering is because Cain did not do what was "right." The Lord only requires something from an individual after He has given that person clear instructions and has empowered them with the ability to perform the instructions.

Clearly, the Lord must have given both Cain and Abel instructions on the specific offering they were to give. The wording in the Scripture suggests Cain knew what he was supposed to give and had the ability to give it, but he chose not to. He didn't do what was right and because he didn't do what was right, his offering was not favored.

This is the first mention of giving in the Bible. Most interpreters of Scripture believe we should place a special emphasis on passages where principles are first mentioned. Here, God required a specific offering. He did not accept any offering; He accepted the specific one. Now I must reconcile that from the beginning God had specific requirements for some offerings. In response to presenting the required offering, Abel received favor.

Anytime the Lord prompts you to give something specific, He is positioning you for favor in your life. That specific offering might be to an individual, an organization or a church or ministry. It might be in the form of finances or rendering your sweat equity to help. However and wherever the offering is planted, your obedience will unleash a downpour of God's favor.

In Genesis 15, Abram wanted assurance that the promise the Lord made him would actually materialize. During their discourse, God required Abram to offer a specific offering. Abram did as the Lord asked, and He reassured Abram of His previous promise. So there are times when God will require a specific offering.

> *For I am the Lord, I change not...*
> —Malachi 3:6a

The Lord tells us He does not change. God's character is consistent. You will find Him making a promise to a person or group of people in multiple Scriptures. Many of those promises are conditional. In other words, they require an action on the part of man to "trigger" the promise. If we do our part, God will do His.

> *"Bring ye all the tithes into the storehouse, that there may be meat in mine house, and prove me now herewith," saith the Lord of hosts, "if I will not open you the windows of heaven, and pour you out a blessing, that there shall not be room enough to receive it.*
> *And I will rebuke the devourer for your sakes, and he shall not destroy the fruits of your ground; neither shall your vine cast her fruit before the time in the field,"*
> *saith the Lord of hosts.*
> —Malachi 3:10-11

When people who are in covenant with God bring tithes, He will respond by pouring out a blessing and rebuking the devourer. Once again, the tithe is a specific, required offering to get a predictable response from the Lord.

I am seeing a pattern.

When someone brings an offering God has specified and required, that same person will receive a response from God. Abel brought such a sacrifice, and he received favor. Abram did the same and received reassurance of a promise. According to Malachi, when people bring a similar tithe, they can expect a blessing and protection from God.

Of course, the Lord accepts "freewill" offerings— offerings where the giver determines what he will give and how much. The Bible is filled with examples of freewill offerings. So, I am not discouraging freely giving to God. But there are also offerings where God requires something specific.

WHAT IS A TITHE?

Christians who want to please God with their giving should study tithing. In this book, you have read the word "tithe" several times, but what is a tithe anyway?

Tithe as written in the Hebrew language means "tenth" or "tenth part." The dictionary defines the word "tithe" as "one tenth of annual earnings given for the support of the church and clergy."

When produce was harvested in days of old, people would count their yield and a tenth went to God. Ten percent means the tenth part of anything. Today we offer 10 percent of our gross income as our tithe.

The principle of giving one-tenth should be carried over to the New Testament as giving to the church is a belief held by many Christians. Yet most Christians who tithe do so simply because they respect the Old Testament principle and find it a helpful place to begin.

Billy Graham, the great and well-respected, twentieth-century evangelist, said, "We have found in our own home, as have thousands of others, that God's blessing upon the nine-tenths, when we tithe, helps it to go farther than ten-tenths without His blessing."

The question "Are Christians obligated to tithe?" should be answered by deeper questions. What has priority in our lives? Is Christ really first, or do we put ourselves and our own desires ahead of Him? When a believer tithes by bringing 10 percent of their gross income for the support of the church, he is proving God is first on his priority list.

> *But seek ye first the kingdom of God.*
> —Mathew 6:33a

Seeking first the kingdom of God means to make it your top priority. The kingdom of God should take precedence over every other concern we have in life. We should give it priority over food, clothing and shelter. Radical!

Jesus said in the remainder of Matthew 6:33 that when we make the kingdom a priority then "all these things will be added." So, when we give the kingdom precedence all other concerns will be met.

Whatever is a top priority in your life will have your heart. If it's your family then your family has your heart. If it's your job then—you guessed it—your employment has your heart.

> *For where your treasure is, there will your heart be also.*
> —Matthew 6:21

Catch this important point: Your heart can be found simply by locating your treasure. If I want to know where my heart really is, I look for the things I treasure the most.

Treasure is another word for "financial investment." So look at the verse above like this: Where my financial investment is, there is my heart. I prove God is first on my priority list by making financial investments into His kingdom.

Do we really want to invite God to intervene in our finances? After all, by employing the principle of tithing, we give God permission to intervene in our financial affairs!

OBLIGATION OR HONOR

Honor the LORD with thy substance, and with the firstfruits of all thine increase.

—Proverbs 3:9

As you receive your increase—whether it is an increase in finances or an increase in time—it is wise to recognize that it came to you by the hand of the Lord. In response, you should give a dedicated portion back to Him.

According to Proverbs 3:9, that is how God is honored. This is an irrefutable principle. If you view tithing as an obligation then you will miss the entire purpose of giving the tenth. One method God has prescribed in His Word to honor Him is to give a tenth of your increase back to Him. Wow, that means tithing is a method to honor God!

The Principle of Tithing

And the king of Sodom went out to meet him after his return from the slaughter of Chedorlaomer, and of the kings that were with him, at the valley of Shaveh, which is the king's dale. And Melchizedek king of Salem brought forth bread and wine: and he was the priest of the most high God. And he blessed him, and said, "Blessed be Abram of the most high God, possessor of heaven and earth: And blessed be the most high God, which hath delivered thine enemies into thy hand. And he gave him tithes of all."

—Genesis 14:17-20

Here, Genesis 14 records Abram returning from the war of the kings to free his nephew Lot. Abram was successful at liberating Lot from captivity, and he defeated multiple kings in doing so. With each defeat, Abram collected "spoils of war."

As Abram returns with the spoils of war, he locates Melchizedek, who was a king and a priest. Abram gives Melchizedek tithes of all his earnings. As I mentioned in chapter two, at this point there was no law or commandment to tithe. Abram is not tithing by law; he is tithing by principle.

Before the law, tithes were commonly given as a matter of principle.

Several theologians have researched this passage thoroughly. They have uncovered a popular tradition during this time that required those victorious in war to pay tithes to the deity they worshipped. Tithes were paid to pagan gods, idol gods or any other item a person worshipped. If this research is to be trusted—and I see no basis to doubt it—then it stands to reason it was a common practice to pay tithes by principle.

These nations firmly believed their deity assisted, or at least made it possible, for the victor to win the battle. They attributed their success to their deity. Tithing was a public way to honor their deity for giving them the victory.

We can conclude, then, that Abram wanted to do the same—to honor the true and living God for his success by giving tithes to Melchizedek. In return, Melchizedek confers a blessing on Abram. This strengthens my belief in the principle of tithing because I believe everything I have is because of God's hand in my life. Therefore, I honor Him every time I am increased by returning the tithe.

We have discussed the principle of tithing several times before, but what is a principle anyway? A "principle" is an established truth concerning the order of God and the spiritual laws that influence life's situations.

Principles are simple yet powerful models that help us understand how the world works. Principles generate the same results each and every time no matter where they are used, no matter when they are used, no matter who uses them. Principles work when you work them!

Gravity is a principle. When you wake up in the morning, your feet always fall to the floor as you exit your bed rather than float to the ceiling. Why? Because of the principle of gravity.

Friction is a principle in physics. It states that any object in motion will create friction when it is opposed by another object. The principle of friction is always at work!

Principles don't wear out. Principles don't rust out. Principles don't give out. Principles are tireless and timeless. They work when you work them!

In our environment, there are multiple circles of influence or "worlds," such as:

The scientific world, which functions by scientific principles.

The musical world, which has its own principles.

The spiritual world, which functions by spiritual principles.

Spiritual principles always outweigh and overrule all other principles. Everything you see in the natural realm came from the spiritual realm. Spiritual principles are eternal principles. Always place more respect on spiritual principles than any other.

PRINCIPLES PRODUCE PREDICTABLE RESULTS!

> *Give, and it shall be given unto you; good measure, pressed down, and shaken together, and running over, shall men give into your bosom. For with the same measure that ye mete withal it shall be measured to you again.*
> —Luke 6:38

One spiritual principle that I apply to multiple areas of my life is the principle of reciprocity, referred to here in Luke 6:38. In layman's terms: "What you give out is what will come back to you."

Some people call it "karma." Some say, "What goes around comes around." These all refer to this one principle: reciprocity.

I apply this to many areas of my life. I apply it to how I treat others. If I simply treat people with love, care, concern and tenderness then I can expect to be treated with the same.

Now I am astute enough to know I will meet mean people in my life. Truth be told, we all will. And yet, during critical times, many people have extended mercy and shown compassion toward me. I attribute this demonstration of kindness to the prior seed that was sown.

I apply this principle of reciprocity in my marriage. At the time of this writing, my wife and I have been married for over thirty-two years! Anyone who is married or has been married will tell you that every day is not filled with roses.

But if you want a long-lasting, fulfilling relationship you must be willing to make some sacrifices. According to the principle of reciprocity, whatever I give out will come back. Therefore, I make intentional acts of sacrifice on purpose. I will do something I don't necessarily like to do, but my wife wants me to do it with her.

In return, I have seen my wife do things she did not necessarily enjoy only because I wanted her with me. The principle of reciprocity at work! What I gave out came back to me.

Why don't you try it? If you want some joy in your life, try giving joy to others and watch it come back to you. You will be intentionally enacting the principle of reciprocity.

Just like gravity, friction and reciprocity are principles, tithing is a principle also. According to Malachi 3:8-12, when a person in covenant with God tithes from all his income, he can expect a supernatural blessing as well as supernatural protection from God.

[6]

The Purpose of Tithing

The principle of tithing has three primary purposes:
- To honor God for His material gifts
- To support local church, ministries and missions financially
- To give God permission to intervene in our finances

ABRAM HONORED GOD BY TITHING.

When Abram tithed by principle to Melchizedek, he was honoring God for using him to free his nephew Lot from captivity. He publicly thanked God for strength, favor, ability and might and declared that without God's help, he could not have done what he did.

And all the tithe of the land, whether of the seed of the
land, or of the fruit of the tree, is the Lord's:
it is holy unto the Lord.

—Leviticus 27:30

Yes, Leviticus records "the law." But this particular Scripture cannot be overlooked. As a matter of spiritual principle, God views the tithe as His, which means He owns it. Sometimes it's hard to understand how God can claim ownership of something in your possession.

Approximately twenty years ago, my wife was involved in an automobile accident. Thank God she was not severely injured. As a matter of fact, the responding EMTs checked her out and released her to go home with the instruction to see a physician later to make sure everything was all right.

The car, unfortunately, did not fare as well. The insurance company totaled it.

Well, that meant we needed a replacement vehicle. A couple days later, we drove to a car dealer to begin our search. My wife soon found a vehicle she liked. Just the right color, interior, accessories ... the whole thing.

There was only one problem. We did not have the money for a down payment to bring the monthly installments into our budgetary range. Though the insurance check was on the way, we had yet to receive it. I told the salesperson we would return to complete the deal once we received the insurance check.

But the dealer really wanted to move the vehicle that night. They made us an offer to lease it on payments within our budget.

I was amazed because, at first, they requested $1,500 down to seal the deal. Again, I told him we didn't have it and would have to wait.

About ten minutes later, the salesman returned and said, "Congratulations on your new vehicle!"

That night we signed the lease and drove our new car off the lot. The payments were within our budget, and we didn't have to put any money down! At the time, it was very uncommon to have a "sign and drive" lease agreement.

For three years, we drove that vehicle like we owned it. We paid for the oil changes, tire rotations and any other maintenance required. We paid for the registration costs. We paid for the gasoline. To someone who didn't know the details of the agreement there was no way to know we did not own the vehicle. But it was a leased vehicle.

When the agreement was up, we returned it to the location the leasing company specified because they owned it. For three years, we possessed it but did not own it. It belonged to the leasing company.

That is how God views tithing. He blesses you and I with income. He allows us to possess all our income...but that first 10 percent He claims as His. He owns it even though we possess it and, because He owns it, He has the right to instruct us on where and when to return what He owns. The tithe is the Lord's; it's holy to the Lord. And when those who are in covenant with Him do not tithe, they are not honoring God as they should.

I hope you were able to catch that: The Lord has the right to determine where and when you return His tithe. To walk in full compliance with this principle of tithing, we must return the tithe to the place the Lord has determined (we will discuss that later). Also, we must return the tithe when the Lord has determined.

Upon the first day of the week let every one of you lay by him in store, as God hath prospered him.
—1 Corinthians 16:2

This passage contains a principle that should be applied to all aspects of giving to the Lord, which we find in the phrase "as God hath prospered him."

As you receive income, you should return a tithe to the Lord's house with the same frequency. If your employer distributes your pay every week, then you tithe every week. If your employer pays you every two weeks, then tithe every two weeks. If you receive your pay every month, again, you should tithe accordingly. What if you are self-employed or paid by commission and there is no set "pay day?" In those instances, you return the tithe when your finances increase.

I have known people to withhold their tithes, pay bills with the money and, at a later time, bring what they should have returned from a prior pay period and what they owe from their current pay period. Let me caution you! Delayed obedience is still disobedience.

> *And if a man will at all redeem ought of his tithes, he shall add thereto the fifth part thereof.*
> —Leviticus 27:31

The word "redeem" in the Hebrew language means to deliver, avenge or act as a kinsman. The implication is to "buy back." In this context, though, if one buys back a tithe that belongs to the Lord, that person is actually holding back the tithe because it is already in their possession. From that we can see there is an additional fee assessed for buying back or withholding the tithe from when it was principally due.

The additional fee required by the Lord is to add the "fifth part" to it. I used to think if the tithe is a tenth or 10 percent, then the fifth part is another 5 percent. But my understanding at that time was erroneous.

Today's English version makes it clear that the fifth part is equivalent to 20 percent. Now I get it. If I divide a whole pie into ten pieces and remove one piece, that one piece would equal 10 percent. However, if I were to divide that same pie into five pieces and remove one-fifth, or the fifth part, one-fifth is equal to 20 percent.

Get a hold of that! The additional fee for withholding the tithe is 20 percent. Then you must add the original 10 percent for a total of 30 percent due. I don't know about you, but I would rather return the 10 percent on time than the 30 percent because I withheld the ten. It's a matter of properly honoring God with what He says, when He says it.

The Lord of heaven's armies says to the priests: "A son honors his father, and a servant respects his master. If I am your father and master, where are the honor and respect I deserve? You have shown contempt for my name!"

But you ask, "How have we ever shown contempt for your name?"

"You have shown contempt by offering defiled sacrifices on my altar."

Then you ask, "How have we defiled the sacrifices?"

"You defile them by saying the altar of the LORD deserves no respect. When you give blind animals as sacrifices, isn't that wrong? And isn't it wrong to offer animals that are crippled and diseased? Try giving gifts like that to your governor, and see how pleased he is!" says the LORD of heaven's armies.

"Go ahead, beg God to be merciful to you! But when you bring that kind of offering, why should He show you any favor at all?" asks the LORD of heaven's armies.

"How I wish one of you would shut the Temple doors so that these worthless sacrifices could not be offered! I am not pleased with you," says the LORD of heaven's armies, "and I will not accept your offerings. But my name is honored by people of other nations from morning till night. All around the world they offer sweet incense and pure offerings in honor

of my name. For my name is great among the nations," says the LORD of heaven's armies.

"But you dishonor my name with your actions. By bringing contemptible food, you are saying it's all right to defile the Lord's table. You say, 'It's too hard to serve the Lord,' and you turn up your noses at my commands," says the Lord of heaven's armies. "Think of it! Animals that are stolen and crippled and sick are being presented as offerings! Should I accept from you such offerings as these?" asks the Lord.

—Malachi 1:6-13 (NLT)

In these verses, you can see how God was displeased with the priests for allowing lame, blind and sick animals as acceptable offerings. These animals could not be sold or traded in the marketplace. They had no significant value in society. These were "leftovers."

God said these types of offerings were a dishonor, not an honor. You see, God does not like a leftover offering, as in what we have left after we have paid the rest of our bills. He is honored when we intentionally and purposely return a tithe by principle willing. The tithe pleases God and the tithe honors God! So one purpose of tithing is to properly honor God for His blessing on your life.

Bring ye all the tithes into the storehouse, that there may be meat in mine house.

—Malachi 3:10

TITHING SUPPORTS THE LOCAL CHURCH.

Another purpose of tithing by principle is the financial support of the local church, its ministries and missions. As you can see in the verse above, the Lord calls for tithes to be brought to the "storehouse." The "storehouse" describes the local church.

There are many worthwhile causes and organizations we should support financially. Those who help the homeless need support. Groups that assist with the men and women who have served our country's military should be supported. Major organizations that help when people have been displaced domestically due to fire or natural disasters need financial support. All are worthy causes, yet none of these are qualified to receive tithes because they are not the "storehouse."

Just in case there was some confusion over what He meant when He said "storehouse," the Lord clarified by saying "that there may be meat in mine house…"

"Mine house" and "storehouse" speak of the same place—the house of the Lord or your local church. Deuteronomy 12:5-6 confirms this by describing the place where tithes are to be brought by calling it "the place which the Lord your God shall choose…to put His name…"

Now it says "that there may be meat in mine house." The term "meat" means provision. It infers that it would be sufficient provision to supply enough resources for the ministries of the local church and the minister.

If pastors and churches would teach giving scripturally there would be no need for ancillary fundraising. The local church should not have to rely on selling chicken dinners, or hosting fish fries, bingo nights, or rummage sales for its primary financial support. That primary support should come from the principle of tithing and scriptural giving.

Another purpose of tithing goes back to my prior statement that it gives God permission to intervene in our personal affairs and finances. In the chapter titled "The Intervention Principle," I shared how God must be invited to intervene in man's affairs. The tithe invites God to intervene. As a matter of fact, Malachi 3 records a promise from God to "pour out a blessing" and "rebuke the devourer." Wow, God wants to be personally involved in our lives and specifically our finances. It is the tithe that commits His intervention.

In John 10:10, Jesus says, "The thief comes to steal, kill and destroy…" That sounds like a devourer to me. The evil one's attacks are designed to rob you of what God has promised by attempting to steal your peace, your sound mind, your health and even your covenant of prosperity. He does not want you to enjoy life! He wants to devour it! That is why the Lord says He will rebuke him when we tithe.

From a spiritual perspective, tithing is much better than any home security system ever invented. A home security system can only notify you and the monitoring station when a potential intruder has come into your home. Often, though, the notification comes too late to stop the intruder from entering your residence.

God says He will "rebuke" the devourer. Which means, before the devil, the enemy, that evil one gets an opportunity to steal, kill or destroy, the Lord will stop him right in his tracks. That's getting God to intervene. We will delve into this further in the next chapter.

Our last purpose also comes from Malachi 3:12, which says, "And all nations shall call you blessed..."

When people from diverse nationalities look at your life and observe the challenges you have faced and the obstacles you have overcome, they will declare you are "blessed," acknowledging that you could not have done what you have done without God's help.

According to Malachi, when you tithe the blessing will be so evident to others that they will give God the glory for what He has and is doing in your life. So, here is another purpose of the tithe—that God would receive the glory out of your life!

[7]

The Promise of Tithing

Throughout the Bible, you find numerous promises. According to the website Bible Info, one person counted 3,573 promises in the Bible. Wow. That is a whole lot of promises.

Some of those promises are exclusive, meaning they only apply to the person or group of people to whom they were made. Some of those promises are inclusive and unconditional. Simply put, they are available to everyone without any conditions or required actions on the individual to receive the benefit of the promise. Then there are some that are inclusive and conditional. These apply to anyone who will meet the conditions of the promise.

Take, for instance, those listed in Deuteronomy 28. God makes several promises to bless in multiple ways and even protect anyone who will obey His Word (His statutes and commands). God only commits to fulfill those promises when someone meets the condition of obedience to His Word.

GOD MAKES PROMISES TO STIMULATE OUR FAITH.

Anytime God makes a promise to an individual, He does it to motivate that person's faith. Faith is the currency of the kingdom of God. In the United States of America, the dollar is the currency for the exchange of goods and services. But in the realm of the spirit, faith is the currency used for the exchange. Consider this verse:

> *But without faith it is impossible to please Him: for he that cometh to God must believe that He is, and that He is a rewarder of them that diligently seek Him.*
> —Hebrews 11:6

Here we see several important truths. First, without faith pleasing God is totally impossible. God requires you to use your faith so He can be pleased. Second, when we approach God we must believe in His existence and His ability to work in our lives.

Because God created us, He knows how we function. Humans need motivation to "believe." We don't just believe because something is visible or apparent. Actually, we can see something with our eyes and choose not to believe it. Have you ever seen a magician perform a trick and say to yourself, "I don't believe it"? For humans to believe we need the proper motivation. In steps God. He makes a promise to heal us. Jeremiah 33:6a says, "Behold, I will bring it health and cure, and I will cure them..." It is a promise to stir our faith to believe He will heal us. Once our faith is activated in that area, now He can fulfill His promise to us!

It is the same with tithing. For the principle of tithing to work for your benefit, God makes a promise connected to the tithe so we can have faith for the fulfillment of the promise.

Now, concerning the tithe there are specific promises for those who will meet the condition of tithing according to principle:

> *"Bring ye all the tithes into the storehouse, that there may be meat in mine house, and prove me now herewith," saith the Lord of hosts, "if I will not open you the windows of heaven, and pour you out a blessing, that there shall not be room enough to receive it. And I will rebuke the devourer for your sakes, and he shall not destroy the fruits of your ground; neither shall your vine cast her fruit before the time in the field," saith the Lord of hosts.*
>
> —Malachi 3:10-11

The first promise to those who tithe by principle is found in verse 10: "...if I will not open you the windows of heaven, and pour you out a blessing, that there shall not be room enough to receive it."

THE WINDOWS OF HEAVEN

The King James Version calls them windows, but the NIV uses the term "floodgates." "Floodgates" has more meaning in the context of something being poured out.

I live happily in south Florida, where we have tropical weather systems move through occasionally. Some of these weather systems can dump an enormous amount of rain in a short period of time. When this happens, our area can be subject to flooding.

Well, our water management authorities have constructed floodgates on our rivers and canals to control the level of water and prevent flooding in populated areas. When the meteorologists predict enormous amount of rain, the authorities open the floodgates to release millions of gallons of water from our rivers, streams and canals into the ocean. It is a massive release of water.

When the Lord says He will open the floodgates of heaven, the idea is a massive release of heaven's blessings on an individual. We are not talking about the release of dew or a drizzle amount but an immense quantity all at once!

POUR YOU OUT A BLESSING!

The idea here is that of a large bottle, pitcher or carafe—something used for holding water, juice or any other beverage. As you picture the carafe being "poured out," it would eventually get to the point where nothing remains in it. The pouring out is actually an emptying out. Meaning the carafe is emptied of its contents.

The emptying out of a blessing from heaven is significant. When a lady empties her purse, she turns it upside down with the top open and all of the contents come flowing out of the purse. Anything in it will come out. Nothing is held back!

When the Lord says He will "pour you out a blessing," He is saying it is an emptying out and no blessing will be withheld. Whatever blessing you need will be released to you when you need it and how you need it.

Please catch this Important distinction: A "blessing" is not the material things we call a blessing—the car, the house, the finances or the promotion on your job. These are the effects of the blessing. Think of leaves blowing down a street in the fall. You see the leaves as they move across the pavement and think to yourself, "Wow, look at the wind." In actuality, though, you are not observing the wind at all but the effect the wind has on the leaves. Though the wind is invisible, it is real. You can feel it yet only see its effects. This blessing is just like that. It is invisible and real. The evidence of its reality and presence is the effect or multiple effects it has on your life.

The blessing is an empowerment to succeed, just as a curse is an empowerment to fail. It is an invisible empowerment from heaven that has a positive effect on your life for good things to happen to you and for you. This is what the Lord says will happen when you participate in the principle of tithing.

So here is the first promise: to open the floodgates, releasing a massive amount of empowerment for you to succeed and no type of empowerment will be withheld.

This blessing could be called an "anointing." An anointing, as referenced in the Bible, is a smearing on many times with oil. This smearing on signified God's presence and His power operating in an individual's life. The anointing is literally a spiritual equipping for the believer. This spiritual equipping gives you an ability you did not have previously. You can do things with the anointing that you cannot do without it. So the blessing is both an empowerment and an equipping.

REBUKE THE DEVOURER!

The second promise to the one who will tithe by principle is found in Malachi 3:11: "And I will rebuke the devourer for your sakes, and he shall not destroy the fruits of your ground; neither shall your vine cast her fruit before the time in the field."

I mentioned this promise in the last chapter as we were discussing the purpose of tithing. This time, let's look at it a little closer. A rebuke is a sharp reprimand or correction. The Lord says He will "rebuke the devourer," meaning He will sharply reprimand and correct the enemy.

Jesus said in John 10:10, "The thief cometh not, but for to steal, and to kill, and to destroy." You must realize you have a real enemy and that enemy is extremely serious about stopping the plan of God in your life. Just because you cannot see this enemy with your physical eyes does not mean he isn't real.

Jesus called this enemy "the thief." It implies that this demonic spiritual entity—who is also called the devil, the thief or Satan—does not want you to enjoy everything God has provided for you. But God has a different plan. He will rebuke the devourer when you tithe so you can enjoy His provision.

This rebuke is heavenly protection against an attack. You must understand this, child of God—you are engaged in a spiritual war twenty-four hours a day, seven days a week, 365 days a year. Spiritual warfare for the believer never stops!

Fortunately, you have been given several spiritual weapons to utilize. You have angels who fight for you in the spirit realm. You have the spiritual armor listed in Ephesians 6. Most of all, you have the Lord Himself who will fight for you. Because you are in a constant state of spiritual warfare, you need all the spiritual protection you can get. When God says He will rebuke the devourer, this protection against an attack covers two areas: "the fruit" and "the field."

Fruit is what a tree produces. I am a Floridian, therefore I am accustomed to seeing tropical trees and plants with fruit. Oranges, mangoes, avocados and bananas are plentiful everywhere you go. Fruit, as you know, is the edible or useful part of the plant or tree.

Metaphorically, then, fruit is what you produce that you can use. It can be the result of your work. Your hourly pay or yearly salary can be classified as fruit because it is what you produced and it is useful to you. If you are a business owner and you plan to pass that business down to your children one day, then your fruit could be the business asset.

The protection of the fruit is powerful! There are always things that will attempt to devour what you have worked hard to accomplish. When you have labored for something significant in your life, you never want to see any attempt to take it away. I have seen hurricanes take out homes in a matter of hours. I have seen the stock market lose so much in one day it destroyed people's retirement accounts. But when you tithe, the Lord promises to protect the fruit of your labors!

When I was very young, there was a plant that could be found in almost every yard in south Florida. This particular plant would produce these wonderful-tasting cherries. Oh, how I would love to go out and pick and eat those cherries. Still, you had to be careful because worms also liked those cherries.

As we ate them, we would frequently check for invading worms within the fruit. When a worm was found, the entire cherry was discarded. It's the same when we tithe—the Lord says He will protect the fruit. No more invading worms destroying what we worked so hard to produce!

I have seen destructive things happen to people who tithe. Then, seemingly without hesitation, what appeared to be lost was replaced so quickly it was like it was never gone at all. That's the Lord protecting the fruit.

Also, when the Lord "rebukes the devourer" He protects the "field." Sometimes a farmer's harvest is destroyed because of insects in the ground eating the root system or because of a ground disease or fungus. The agricultural language found in Malachi tells us the Lord will protect our field. With so many enemies attacking the ground, this is important.

Let's apply that to your situation. You work to produce fruit but the place of work and the type of work is essential to your success. The place and type becomes your field. With your tithe, the Lord protects your place of employment and your type of employment. I have personally seen this happen.

At one time, I was working for a large private corporation as a service representative in a specific area. As long as I was with that company, the company and my area were profitable.

After working there for eight years, though, I accepted a full-time ministry position at my local church. Two years later, I went back to my old job just to see everyone and say hello. To my surprise, the office was locked and empty. There was no name next to the office door. I peered through the window and saw what appeared to be the remnants of a cake.

Then it hit me: This local service office had been closed permanently by the corporation. Technology had revolutionized the way they manufactured and serviced their products, so they no longer needed field service offices. Yet while I was there, the Lord protected my employment because of my tithe. He then moved me into a different field before the change in the company.

The tithe protects the fruit, but it also protects the field.

[8]

The Perfect Example of Giving

No matter how many principles we can learn, it is always wonderful when we have a great example to follow as we apply that principle. Since making Jesus my Lord, I have heard many people say, "I want to be like Jesus!" They want to follow His example and apply His principles in a practical way on an everyday basis. I do believe the absolute best example people can follow is Jesus's example.

For God so loved the world, that He gave His only begotten Son, that whosoever believeth in Him should not perish, but have everlasting life.

—John 3:16

When it comes to giving, look at what this verse says about how, what and why God gives. It starts with, "For God so loved the world, that He gave..." Notice for a moment why God gives: God gives because He loves.

This definitely applies to the topic of tithing. To demonstrate our love we give. As I mentioned earlier, my wife and I have been married for more than three decades. I adore my wife and because I adore her, I love to demonstrate my feelings by being generous to her. When you really love someone or something you receive pleasure from giving. I've heard it said that actions speak louder than words. Therefore, we should follow God's example and let our giving be an extension of our love.

The verse goes on: " ...He gave his only begotten Son..."

Can you imagine having only one son then, to help all humanity, you make the decision to give that son away? I am a father and cannot imagine giving my son away. This lets me know that God always gives His best.

Wow. What an example to follow! When we give and to whomever we give, it should always be our best. Sometimes we give and what we give is not our worst, but it is also definitely not our finest. Imagine the sense of fulfillment we would discover if we only gave the best we have to offer. That is what that 10 percent represents!

Not only does God give His best, but God gives His best sacrificially. A sacrifice is something extraordinary. It is surrendering something we prize in exchange for something we believe has far greater worth. Think about that! God surrendered His Son because He placed a higher claim on our souls.

Apply that to the principle of tithing. When we tithe we are surrendering something prized, which is 10 percent of our gross income, for the promise that has a higher claim.

Let's go further in the verse. The next section states, "...that whosoever believeth in Him should not perish..."

Another reason God gives is so others can benefit from the gift given. It is an act of unselfishness when we give for the sake of others. The same is true with our money. Tithing benefits the local church, which in turn provides ministry for those who are hurting and in need.

One more point we can extract from that famous verse: God gives expecting a return. The Lord gave His Son as a sacrifice anticipating we will accept that gift and come into a relationship with Him. We commonly call people who receive Jesus as Savior "the harvest of souls." Well, a harvest is simply a return on an invested seed. It is quite okay to expect to receive something from our giving because God expects to receive us as a result of His gift.

[9]

Make A Decision

*"And if it seem evil unto you to serve the LORD, choose
you this day whom ye will serve; whether the gods which your
fathers served that were on the other side of the flood, or the
gods of the Amorites, in whose land ye dwell: but as for me
and my house, we will serve the LORD."*

—Joshua 24:15

Yes, it is time for you to make a choice! You must
choose how you will serve God. Will you serve God
based upon your humanly conceived ideas? Will you
serve Him based on ideas and philosophies derived
from secular humanism? Will you serve Him based on
concepts socially accepted at the current time? Or will
you choose to serve God based upon scriptural principles?

It's time to make a decision!

Will you decide to believe tithing is not for today because it is included in "the law"? Will you decide to believe tithing is just for those who were in the Old Testament? Will you decide to believe that because we are in the dispensation of "grace" tithing does not apply to us? Or will you decide the principle of tithing is valid for any time period and for anyone who will get involved with that principle?

In this book, you have read the scriptural evidence proving the principle of tithing began at least four hundred years before the Mosaic Law was given. Yes, this principle was included in the Mosaic Law, so those who were under that dispensation could be "blessed" by its promises. Yet Jesus tells us in Matthew that this principle should not be "undone" or done away with.

You may have noticed I did not address the curse of not tithing. If a blessing is an empowerment to succeed then a curse is an empowerment to fail! I did not address the curse because when you understand the truth of the principle of tithing you should not desire to have any negative consequences. You should choose to participate with this scripturally ordained principle.

Why should you tithe? You tithe to take part in a scriptural kingdom principle that impacts your natural situation and is still in operation today. You tithe to honor God for His blessing. You tithe to permit God to intervene in your finances and your life. You tithe to trigger the floodgates of heaven's blessing to be released into your life.

You tithe to permit God to rebuke the devourer and protect your fruit and your field. You tithe to scripturally support your local church with your finances. You tithe to follow God's example of principled giving. You tithe because of all of the positive benefits the Lord has promised would be yours by obeying this principle.

Instead of asking, "Why should I tithe?" maybe the real question is, "Why shouldn't I tithe?"

Scripture Index

ABOUT THE AUTHOR

An anointed teacher and visionary leader, Dr. Henry D. Daniels is the senior pastor and founder of Cornerstone Christian Center Church in Pembroke Pines and Hollywood, Florida.

Dr. Daniels received the vision of Cornerstone in 1995. The Lord instructed him to build and strengthen strong families by teaching the Word of God, so the families would make a global impact in their communities.

In August of 2000, Cornerstone Community Church of South Florida, held its first worship service at A. C. Perry Elementary School in Miramar, Florida, with over 100 persons in attendance. The ministry blossomed and grew and in July of 2001, Cornerstone relocated to a location in Pembroke Pines, Florida. Cornerstone Community Church of South Florida became Cornerstone Christian Center Church in August of 2004. Then in June of 2006, the ministry acquired its ministry location in Hollywood, Florida. Cornerstone has now grown to over 1,700 members.

Dr. Daniels and his wife Teresa, are partners together in marriage and in ministry. Henry Daniels holds a Bachelor of Arts in Christian Education. In addition, Henry & Teresa Daniels received Doctor of Divinity degrees from St. Thomas Christian College in Jacksonville, Florida.

Prayer of Salvation

The most important decision a person can make is to receive Jesus as Lord and Savior. Jesus laid down His life and rose again so we could spend eternity with Him in Heaven. If you would like to receive Jesus and become born again, pray this prayer from your heart:

Heavenly Father, I come to you admitting I am a sinner. I ask You to cleanse me of all unrighteousness. I believe Jesus died on the cross for my sin and rose again from the dead. I call on the name of Jesus to be my Savior and Lord. I ask You to fill me with the power of the Holy Spirit. I declare right now, I am a child of God, free from sin and I am saved in Jesus' name, Amen.

If you have prayed this prayer to receive Jesus as your Savior, or if this book has changed your life, we would like to hear from you. Please write us at:

Orange Publishers
15757 Pines Blvd. Suite 245
Pembroke Pines, Florida 33027

To Contact Dr. Henry D. Daniels write to:

Dr. Henry D. Daniels
15757 Pines Blvd. Suite 245
Pembroke Pines, Florida 33027

CPSIA information can be obtained
at www.ICGtesting.com
Printed in the USA
LVHW021024110620
657585LV00007B/519